Written by Amy Wilson

Edited by Philippa Wingate
Designed by Zoe Quayle
Production by Joanne Rooke
Picture Research by Judith Palmer

Picture Acknowledgements
Vince Dolman/RetnaUK: Front cover
Getty Images: Back cover

Dave Nelson/expresspictures.com: pages 38/39, 55, 57
Humphrey Nemar/expresspictures.com: pages 19, 34, 59
SMEA/LFI: page 12
PA Photos: pages 6, 46/47
Patrick Catler/RetnaUK: pages 10, 14
Lee Floyd/RetnaUK: pages 24/25, 52/53
Rob Watkins/RetnaUK: pages 8/9
REX FEATURES: page 21
Geoff Robinson/REX FEATURES: page 29
Brian Rasic/REX FEATURES: pages 2/3, 17, 30/31, 45, 62/63
Richard Young/REX FEATURES: page 36

First published in Great Britain in 2004 by Buster Books,
an imprint of Michael O'Mara Books Ltd,
9 Lion Yard, Tremadoc Road,
London SW4 7NQ

A CIP catalogue record for this book is available from the British Library.

ISBN: 1-904613-71-3

3 5 7 9 10 8 6 4 2

Printed and bound in Italy by L.E.G.O.

BUSTED

Unauthorized

Annual 2005

Contents

Introduction

BUSTED

It's been a phenomenal year for Busted. With the release of their second album, *A Present for Everyone*, Charlie Simpson, Matt Jay and James Bourne have confirmed their place at the heart of the British pop scene.

Their stellar career kicked off in 2002 and has continued to escalate this year with yet more number-one singles.

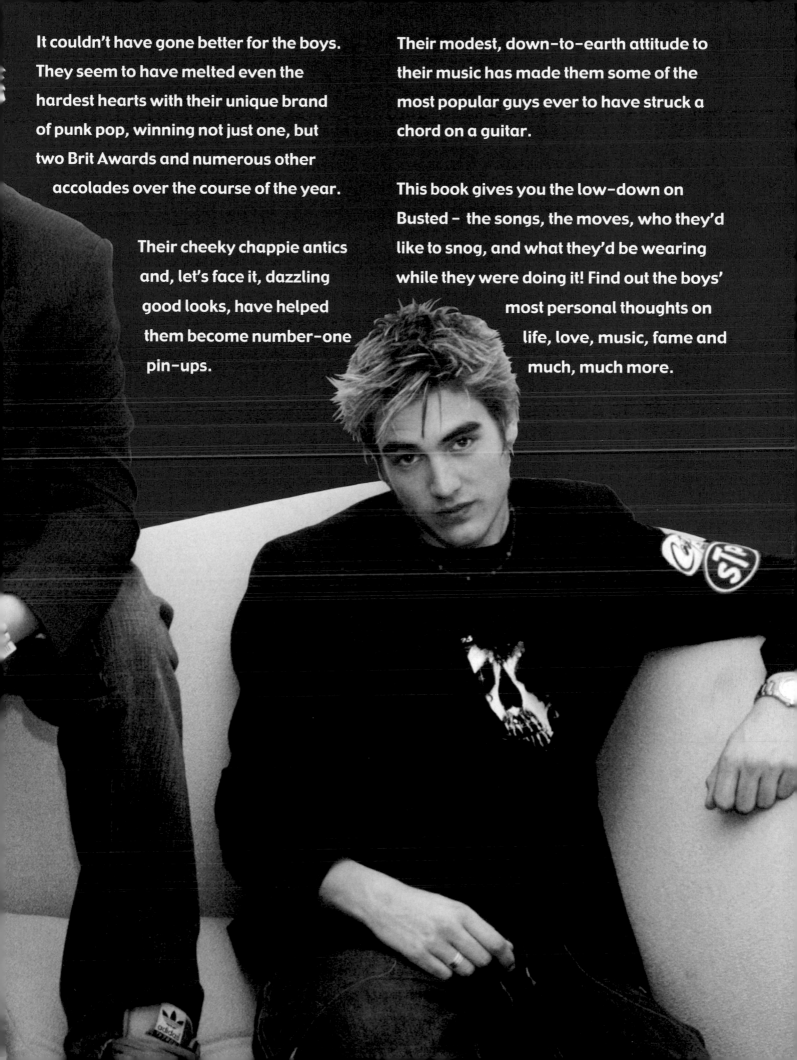

It couldn't have gone better for the boys. They seem to have melted even the hardest hearts with their unique brand of punk pop, winning not just one, but two Brit Awards and numerous other accolades over the course of the year.

Their cheeky chappie antics and, let's face it, dazzling good looks, have helped them become number-one pin-ups.

Their modest, down-to-earth attitude to their music has made them some of the most popular guys ever to have struck a chord on a guitar.

This book gives you the low-down on Busted – the songs, the moves, who they'd like to snog, and what they'd be wearing while they were doing it! Find out the boys' most personal thoughts on life, love, music, fame and much, much more.

JAMES BUSTED

Profile

Name: James Bourne

Date of birth: 13 September 1983

School: Alleyn Court School, Southend-on-Sea, Essex

Family: Two brothers, Chris and Nick, and a sister called Mel

Facial characteristics: Round cheeks, bright blue eyes, and a massive, cheeky grin

Favourite colour: Blue

Star sign: Virgo – which means he's reliable, hard-working, and a bit of a perfectionist.

Known as: The songwriter. The intelligent one (although he forgets to pay his bills). And he just loves farting!

Loves: Playing pool, having a laugh with his mates back home in Southend-on-Sea, ping-pong and pancakes.

Hates: His old school uniform – it had pink stripes and he has never been able to live it down.

And finally: He once thought a slug was a wine gum and ate it. It was on the floor of his bedroom and he was hungry. Gross!

10

Did you know...?

James is the kind of boy your mum would love you to bring home – but he's got a few surprises up his sleeve:

• James admits he's not too good with the whole changing sheets thing: "I tried to make up my own bed once and it took me two hours. The pillows were easy, but the duvet was a two-man job!"

• In James World – "There would be lots of music everywhere. You would have to put on head-phones if you didn't want to listen to it! And the streets would be made of food so you could eat anything, anywhere."

• Once James forgot to pay his electricity bill. Leading a busy pop-star life meant he just didn't get around to dealing with it, so he suddenly found himself back at his flat with no power. Now he has a meter with a top-up card. Very showbiz!

• He's been known to be a little light-fingered – strictly by accident, of course. "I took too many of those penny sweets. I said I had 50 pence-worth, but I found a few extra at the bottom of the bag. That haunted me for weeks after!" Ah, he's a bit of a sweetie himself.

• James doesn't always have the time to be mummy's little angel. "My mum rang me the other day and I couldn't speak to her, so she got annoyed," he admits.

• Charlie thinks James is the maddest person he has ever known.

• James once said he wanted plastic surgery to get ears like an elf. Very *Lord of the Rings*!

• He would drink his own wee for £30,000!

MATT

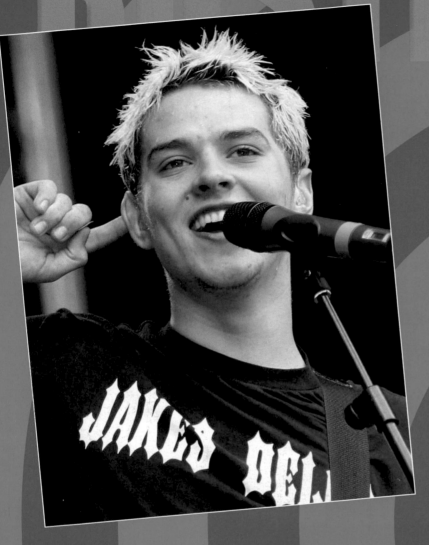

Profile

Name:	Matt Jay
Date of birth:	8 May 1983
School:	Sylvia Young Theatre School, London
Family:	A brother, Darren, and a sister called Amanda
Facial characteristics:	Pointy chin and naughty, twinkling, dark eyes
Favourite colour:	Red

Star sign: Taurus – which means he's patient and kind, with a warm heart. On the other hand, he can be rather stubborn and just a tad possessive.

Known as: The mischievous one, always playing practical jokes. For some reason, he loves throwing things out of windows – bananas, TVs, toasters.

Loves: Madness (the band, that is!) and flirting.

Hates: People who take themselves too seriously, and cats.

And finally: By the age of ten, Matt had broken twenty-eight bones in his body. He puts it down to jumping out of trees and climbing walls.

Did you know...?

Everyone knows that Matt has a reputation for being a practical joker, but here are a few things you might not know:

• One of Matt's biggest ambitions is to share the stage with his heroes, Blink 182. He admits to being just a bit obsessed with the band.

• He once broke the ice with a girl by asking her if she had farted. Hmm... what a charmer.

• His favourite pick-me-up after a hard night partying is bangers, mash and onion gravy.

• When he was six, he had warts on his knee, and terrorized the girl who sat next to him at school by rubbing them against her. Ewww!

• Matt would love to be a peregrine falcon.

• He's a fan of *Pop Idol* star Darius – "He's a nice guy, actually. We see him quite a lot. He's a really top guy. Very tall. We thought Charlie was tall, but Darius is extremely tall."

• Matt hates the wind and rain. If he could choose, he would only have two types of weather – sunny or snowy.

• The worst job he ever had was cutting grass for a water company around massive open-top tanks filled with human poo. Gross!

• Matt once roller-skated over his own hand while he was doing a trick, and broke four of his fingers.

• He's always getting moaned at for being fidgety, and he only sleeps for five hours a night, tops.

• Matt wanted to be a fireman when he was younger. He thought the yellow hats were cool.

CHARLIE

Profile

Name: Charlie Simpson

Date of birth: 7 June 1985

School: Uppingham Public School, Rutland

Family: Two older brothers, Will and Ed

Facial characteristics: Chiselled good looks, endearing gap between his front teeth. Oh, and eyebrows! Need we say more?

Favourite colour: Green

Star sign: Gemini – which means he's witty, a bit of a live wire. Good with words, but not so good with money. Easily bored.

Known as: The posh one, always being teased about his cut-glass vowels. The tall one – 6ft 2ins at the last count!

Loves: His first electric guitar which he got when he was ten years old and is still playing on stage.

Hates: Sweet popcorn and fish.

And finally: James and Matt thought Charlie was Dutch when they first met him.

14

Did you know...?

Charlie is one supercool guy. With his swoonsome good looks and posh-boy image, he's pretty perfect, but even Charlie has a few things he'd rather you didn't know:

• He weed his pants once and his parents caught it on camera. Mind you, he was only four years old at the time.

• On Planet Charlie there would be no fish, but lots of Britney lookalikes.

• He hates it when people laugh at things he says just to be polite.

• Charlie has a bit of a soft spot for cheerleaders. He reckons they'd be good to party with.

• Even Charlie has had the odd love-life fiasco – "I crashed and burned once in my life," he admits. "It was at a disco, and I went up to this girl and said 'Do you want to dance?' and she said 'Yes, just let me get my friends.'"

• His mum used to call him Farley when he was little, because he loved Farley's Rusks so much.

• Charlie's first band was called Natural Disasters. He was twelve years old when it was formed and his headmaster came up with the name.

• He used to have a comfort blanket called Night-Night. Bless.

• He once got athlete's foot and his foot went all crusty and manky. Gross!

• Charlie is well chuffed with the way the band sounds – "The way Busted is now is brilliant. It's kind of pop music but with guitar heaviness," he enthuses.

THE REAL STORY
BUSTED

The last two years have seen Busted become so huge it's almost impossible to imagine the world without them. But every story has a beginning. Here's the low-down on how Busted came to be – from how they met and what they thought of each other, to what makes them such good friends.

Matt's and James's first official meeting was at James's house in 2001, but they had already crossed paths at auditions and gigs.

The thing Matt remembers most about the meeting was James's house – "My first impression was, 'This is bloody nice, I wouldn't mind a bit of this.'"

The pair began songwriting, but soon decided they needed a third member. They put an ad in *NME* magazine and along came Charlie. Matt remembers, "Charlie's audition was perfect. We thought he'd been sent from heaven."

Charlie, sixteen at the time, was still at school and only made it to the auditions because of his music teacher, who told him –

"Go down to London and join a band."

Babe-magnet Charlie admits he was actually crouching down during their first photoshoot, because he was worried he would look too tall. Awww... bless him.

After hauling themselves around loads of record companies, and even getting a good reaction from music supremo and *Pop Idol* baddie Simon Cowell, the boys were signed by Universal Records in 2002.

Charlie says the early days seemed crazy because it all happened so fast – "When we started out, I was a bit intimidated," he admits. "It was all new and weird. It was like, 'People are interviewing me. Why the hell do they care?' But now it's great."

From the start, the boys have been the best of friends. They're always seen out together. Once they were spotted partying with a man in a monkey suit!

They know absolutely everything about each other, the good bits and the bad.

While Charlie is the messy one (according to Matt), James is the dirtiest – "James can go four days without a shower," says Matt. "When we're on tour, I always share a room with Charlie. Now you know why!" Charlie remembers – "Once James sneezed, and he thought it was funny to leave the snot dripping from his nose."

James has more endearing habits than bad ones, however. He has a fab American accent, and he's rather good at the old songwriting lark. He gets his own back on the other two by scaring the pants off them – "We wind each other up," he says. "If we're on a plane and there's a bit of turbulence, I stare at Charlie in a freaky way. It makes him nervous."

Matt has a firm reputation as a party animal, but he's very organized and a self-confessed list-lover. He's pretty good around the house too. He's shown James how to use the dishwasher thirteen times!

Charlie says he's the most romantic of the boys, and the others agree. Aww!

Matt reckons Charlie is a bit of a swan – "Charlie was the ugly duckling of the band. Before 'What I Go To School For', he was really quiet and just lurked around in the background. Now he's blossomed and grown into a beautiful swan."

If either Matt or Charlie left Busted, James would replace them with Avril Lavigne.

WHAT THEY SAY
BUSTED

2004 has really been Busted's year. Everyone has fallen in love with them, and that goes for some of the harshest critics out there. The boys seem to have won everybody over!

What the celebrities say

Lemar: "I like Busted. They've got good rock/pop songs and they perform them really well."

Fatman Scoop: "Busted are awesome! I'd love to do a duet with them."

Shane from Westlife: "I think they're the best new pop group around."

What the media says

Mizz: "These boys've got talent – and they look good, too!"

The *Guardian:* "Fizzily effective, scrubbed-clean pop-punk."

Music Week: "Already Britain's best pop act, by some distance."

Sneak: "There's much more to Busted than loud one-liners."

Sugar: "We can't stop humming along to them."

Teen Now (reviewing 'Air Hostess'): "Another classic pop tune in which they show their heartfelt appreciation for air hostesses."

The *Daily Telegraph:* "Pop at its shiniest, stupidest best."

The *Independent:* "Busted are phenomenally successful... a rollicking, clean, fun (time) for all the family."

MTV Asia: "Busted have done really well because of having a really good attitude to working over here... Busted's music has done so well because it's so different from everything else that has been offered. We're expecting them to be a really big act over here for the next few years."

ALL MIXED UP
BUSTED

Rearrange these letters to find some essential Busted words.
You'll find the answers at the bottom of the page.

1. HSTOARSSIE

2. EENIDETWASRDCHGHD

3. TGOOTISROFLOHCHOWA

4. SHESVKPOIROERA

5. LGOHYSRIPC

6. YNTRBIE

7. TJAMATY

8. JEBMAERNOUS

(a)   (b)   (c)

Who's who?

20

BUSTED A TO Z

BUSTED

This comprehensive A-to-Z guide on Matt, James and Charlie will reveal something that even their greatest fans didn't know...

A is for ANIMALS. The boys may be party animals, but they've also got a soft spot for the real thing. Matt just adores dogs, and Charlie used to have a rabbit called Snow White and two guinea-pigs, Bill and Ben.

B is for BLING. The Busted crew have their fair share of bling-bling, and luxury living. Even when they're on tour they have jacuzzis and all the latest technology at their fingertips, thanks to their massive tour bus.

C is for CASH. They admit they're not short of a bob or two following all their successes. Matt is particularly close to his dosh. He often wakes up with money all over him, literally. His bed is always full of coins, because he lies on it with his jeans on and the coins in his pockets fall out. When he wakes up he says there's often a coin stuck to his chest. Mmmm, lucky coin!

D is for DREAMS. Matt has some very odd dreams. Once he dreamt he was wobbling his front teeth and the entire front of his jaw fell off. Sounds more like a nightmare!

E is for ELECTRIC. James once gave himself a bit of a shock (literally) when he accidentally spat into his microphone. Fortunately it was nothing serious, but he still got a little frazzled over the incident.

F is for FITNESS. They're all pretty fit to look at, but apparently they aren't fit in a sporty way. Matt admits he's not exactly an exercise buff - "I'm so bad at that sort of stuff. I never go to the gym, ever!"

G is for GAME ON. James takes his ping-pong table on tour, and has even managed to get Justin from The Darkness to play with him.

H is for HITS. They've had their fair share of hits over the last year, but they've still got their favourites. 'Crashed the Wedding' and 'Nerdy' are Charlie's favourite tracks to perform live.

I is for IDOLS. Charlie, Matt and James are pop idols themselves, but Charlie hates all the reality music TV shows and he'd like to start a campaign against them. Bet that wouldn't make him popular with Simon Cowell!

J is for JUSTIN. The boys are all fans of Mr Timberlake, and Charlie says he'd love to do a duet with him.

K is for KYLIE. James reckons she's so small he could put her in his pocket. Well, he does have fairly large pockets.

L is for LOOKING FORWARD. Charlie reckons the year 3000 will be just like it is in futuristic films, with high buildings and fast cars – and ladies with three breasts. Hmm…

M is for MCFLY. Busted have shown the McFly boys the way to stardom. Matt says – "They're great guys, immensely talented and very cool. There's no doubt they're going to be huge."

N is for NAUGHTY. Well, nobody's perfect! All three of the Busted hunks have pulled stunts in their time. Matt once told a girl he'd written a song when he hadn't at all. He'd just played a cover version. Of course, that was before he became a megastar.

O is for OUCH. James burnt his tongue when a spark from a firework flew right into his mouth during the Busted tour in Dublin.

P is for PYJAMAS. James doesn't wear them. He used to have some Superman pjs, but he stopped wearing them when he was six. Now you'll find him in boxers and a T–shirt.

Q is for QUIRKY. James has some rather strange ways. He silently mouths everything he says after he's spoken (bizarre!), and he once had a hamster called Hump–Three, because it had three lumps on its back.

R is for ROBOTS. They'd love to get one. James reckons a robot guitar would be cool, because it could fix and tune itself.

S is for SNOGTASTIC. Thousands of girls would give their right arm to lock lips with these guys. And the boys aren't exactly averse to a bit of kissing action either. Charlie reckons he's snogged 100 girls, and Matt and James once snogged the same girl. Matt started seeing her at school and then James had an audition with her where he had to kiss her.

T is for TRAVEL. They do plenty of travelling, but fortunately James loves service stations – "The best ones have a McDonald's on one side, and a KFC on the other!" he says.

U is for UNCENSORED. Charlie says the only showbiz person he doesn't like is Louis Walsh, because he said the boys were rubbish and that they'd get dropped.

V is for VINNIE JONES. The football star turned actor is Matt's hero. He'd rather be a bit of a bad boy like Vinnie than like David Beckham.

W is for WHEELS. James reckons a Porsche is a bit of a girl's car. His favourite is a DeLorean – he saw one in the film *Back To The Future*.

X is for X–RATED. Matt was on a night out with pals when they pulled down his pants!

Y is for YOUNG TALENT. Charlie got his first guitar when he was five – "I just picked it up myself. I got a few lessons, but I play a lot of different instruments – bass, drums, guitar and a bit of piano," he says.

Z is for ZZZZ James likes to fall asleep with the TV on, but that doesn't always make for a good night's sleep – sometimes he is woken up by it in the middle of the night.

NAUGHTY... BUSTED

The boys from Busted are on top of the world. Their albums are selling like hot cakes, their videos rock, and they're on TV more than Cat Deeley. So if they get a little naughty occasionally it's only to be expected. Here are a few examples of just how wild those lads can be:

Matt and James once stood on a shelf in their dressing room to lob bananas out of the window. All well and good, you might say, but the shelf came clattering down and broke the TV.

Charlie admits the Busted boys love a bit of bouncing. They've broken many a bed by bouncing up and down on it too many times.

Matt reckons he can sweet talk his way out of trouble – "If I say something naughty, I say it in a funny way so (girls) don't take offence. I even told a girl her bum looked big in what she was wearing and got away with it."

The band got thrown out of a hotel in Munich after they spent the night partying with Lee Ryan from Blue.

James still feels guilty for his part in a prank that dates back to his school days. One of his classmates was put into a sink during an art class and got a thorough soaking. James didn't do the dunking, but he just stood by and watched. Naughty!

Matt has played a part in a few schoolboy pranks in his time. Two years in a row, he and his mates let down the tyres of the headmaster's car. Not only that, but they put egg and flour all over it! He doesn't recommend it though. He got into loads of trouble because the whole thing was caught on camera.

Charlie once weed in a park next to the London Eye.

Matt reportedly caused £1,500 worth of damage at Birmingham's plush Marriott Hotel when he sent a TV crashing to the pavement – along with a toaster (not so cool). He was so embarrassed about the whole thing afterwards, he paid the hotel loads of money to say sorry. See, he's not such a bad boy really.

BUT NICE!

The troublesome trio can sometimes be a bit of a handful. But they can be real sweethearts too. Here's the softer side they'd rather keep secret:

Matt is pretty good at sharing his hard-earned dough. He once bought a sofa for some of his friends because they didn't have the spare cash, and he bought a Ford Mondeo for his mum. What a mummy's boy!

Charlie is known as the gentleman of the trio, and he's certainly not a slacker. He loves to cook up treats, such as pasta with chicken and white wine, for his nearest and dearest.

Matt is a sweetie in more ways than one. When he was little he used to pick up the dog poo in his nan's garden in exchange for sweets. Wonder if he'd do the same now!

James says one of the most important things he's learnt from being in Busted is to make the most of his time with the people he loves, especially family and friends.

Watch out boys, Matt says no one will ever be good enough for his sister. He's very protective of her.

James is a bit of a paternal dude. He admits he wants to be a young dad, and he's really looking forward to it. What are you waiting for girls?

The Busted boys proved that they really are complete softies when they gave all their spare change to a homeless guy they met on the street one day. Then they invited him back to their hotel suite for a shower and some grub. Bless them!

They might be at the height of their fame, but Matt, Charlie and James still have time for the personal touch. They still make visits to supermarkets and music stores to sign autographs for their fans.

BUSTED LOVE

The boys of Busted may be top-class totty, but are they are rogues or Romeos?

Winsome ways

• Charlie wants to get hitched when he's about twenty-six, so he can be a young dad. But, be gentle with him. Charlie confesses, "I usually get quite involved and serious, so I get hurt badly."

• James's philosophy is, if you want a girl, go and get her.

• Matt has a silver unicorn pendant which a girlfriend bought him. He wears it around his neck and says he will treasure it forever.

• Charlie reckons girls should approach boys more. He's not put off by a pro-active babe.

Hot totty

• James: "I think Sarah Whatmore is looking very fit. I've spoken to her a few times and she's so gorgeous."

• Charlie: "I think Tara Reid would be quite a feisty pillow fighter." Ooh-er!

• Matt: "I've always liked Meg Ryan. I think she's very beautiful, that one."

• Charlie: "Britney's so fit. She really does it for me. Also, Avril's cool, I like Avril Lavigne."

Not so hot

• Matt: "One night, I decided to try some cheesy chat-up lines. I went up to a girl and said, 'Go on, pinch me – I'm real.' She looked at me as if I was a freak and walked off." Matt also got dumped at school when he was still the new boy. The girl told him she'd only gone out with him because she felt sorry for him and didn't want to embarrass him in front of everyone.

• James's biggest blow-out ever came when he forgot a girl's name just before he was about to ask her out. Ouch!

• Charlie: "You do get to meet a lot of girls, but we are just so busy with the Busted schedule, it is hard to start a proper relationship."

What they really want

• Matt is pretty fussy. He needs to know what a girl's top-five albums are and, if she says Fast Food Rockers, she's history.

• Charlie doesn't like girls who drive him crazy. He prefers a girl to look good and act nice.

• James says he doesn't go in for the whole candlelit dinners and red roses routine.

IN THE PUBLIC EYE

BUSTED

This year has been a truly amazing ride for the poptastic trio. With two arena tours, International concerts, number one hits galore and awards coming out of their ears, they've hardly been out of the public eye. The boys have never had things so good.

Busted cleaned up at the Smash Hits Poll Winners' Awards, taking away five prizes including Best Band in the World Ever, Stars of the Year, Best Album, and Best UK Band.

Matt got a boost to his ego when he picked up the Top Pop Mop award for his hair.

Then, of course, there were the Brits. The guys walked away with not one , but two awards – Best Pop Act and Best Breakthrough Act. They said the awards meant a lot to them because they were voted for by Radio 1 listeners.

Busted gave a top performance on the night of the awards ceremony, doing their very own version of The Undertones' 'Teenage Kicks'. After the show, the boys celebrated by getting just a little bit tipsy.

Charlie: "It was amazing to be nominated for three Brits, and to win two out of three is fantastic. It was such a buzz being at the Brits."

James: "The fans are amazing. It's down to them we won our two Brit Awards. We love them."

The lads are so proud of their Brits they're making sure everyone can see them. Charlie wants to get his made into a doorknocker. James wants to prop his bed up with his (he needs two more first, though), and Matt has his in pride of place on the mantelpiece.

At the Capital Radio Awards, in aid of the charity Help a London Child, Busted picked up two awards – London's Favourite UK Group and Best Pop Act.

However, all these amazing awards are not the only things which have pushed the band firmly into the public eye. Numerous hit singles, top-notch performances all over the country, awesome TV appearances and some pretty intense partying, have seen their star-rating go through the roof.

The boys pay the price sometimes, though. It's not very easy to go out and about without being spotted when you're part of one of the hottest pop acts in the country.

James: "We definitely get recognized a lot. For example the other day I was walking past the HMV in Piccadilly Circus and some French kids outside the Trocadero recognized me. We were also recognized by German tourists in France."

Matt: "It doesn't get on our nerves, because most people are really nice. Although sometimes people can come up and demand stuff from you. Like, I get a lot of people saying, 'Wait there, I'm just going to buy a camera.'"

Charlie reckons there are some serious bonuses to being a Busted boy – "I was in a band at school and whenever we played gigs I'd always pull that night. And being in Busted is like that, but worldwide!"

WORDSEARCH BUSTED

U	B	P	O	P	C	J	G	Q	T	N	P
D	A	U	O	I	Q	A	N	A	O	D	U
S	I	B	R	E	L	M	F	M	R	A	R
E	R	L	C	M	U	E	P	A	F	V	E
Y	H	S	H	A	E	S	R	T	E	I	O
V	O	F	A	T	I	M	N	T	E	D	H
J	S	T	R	E	H	I	F	R	S	I	F
S	T	L	L	B	U	S	T	E	D	J	V
B	E	O	I	W	V	S	D	A	O	G	I
N	S	W	E	A	J	U	F	M	V	N	D
V	S	R	N	E	R	D	Y	Y	D	Z	E
E	D	X	O	T	P	Y	K	L	T	A	O

Can you find the following words hidden in the grid above?

DAVID   JAMES

VIDEO   BUSTED

CHARLIE   AIR HOSTESS

MATT   NERDY

POP

ON RECORD BUSTED

The Busted boys aren't ones to keep their traps shut. See for yourself:

Charlie: "I think it would be quite funny to see Marilyn Manson do a cover of anything."

James: "Sometimes I say things on stage and afterwards I think, 'I shouldn't have said that.'"

Matt: "I hate people who snore. I only snore if I'm drunk and lying on my back, but I'm asleep so I can't hear it. When someone snores it's so infuriating, I throw things at them like used socks."

James: "Atomic Kitten are fit!"

Charlie: "I'm not posh. My mum is a school secretary and my dad owns a chartered surveyors company. But one of my brothers plays in the same rugby squad as Prince William, and my parents met him."

Matt: "Kym Marsh is so nice. She's lovely."

James : "If I could have any job in the world, besides being in Busted, I'd like to be the person who does Bart Simpson's voice. If someone asked me what my job was, I'd then be able to say, 'I'm Bart Simpson', and it would be absolutely true."

Matt: "My favourite person to watch is Dannii (Minogue). I watch her when she's not on stage as well."

Charlie: "I loved seeing Chesney Hawkes live, even though the cheese was flying high."

Matt: "MC Harvey or Darius would make good prime ministers."

Charlie: "I'm good with children. I take them for walks. "

James: "Justin Timberlake was really friendly when we met him. All I could think was, 'Why did you dump Britney?' but I didn't say it."

Matt: "I cut grass for a while. I wasn't trained enough to have a lawnmower, so I had to have a strimmer."

Charlie: "I don't dance… I shimmy shimmy around with some drinks, very charming."

Matt: "I think Blazin' Squad are top guys."

STAYING TRUE
BUSTED

They might have a rep for being the raunchiest rule-breakers in town, but the Busted crew still have their feet firmly on the ground. They haven't forgotten their old friends or their families.

Matt spent last Christmas with his family, and says he had a great time. He met a load of the locals, and at New Year threw a massive house party for all his pals – "The whole world seemed to be there!" he says.

James says some people he used to hang out with have gone weird and don't know what to say to him any more. But that's OK, because all his real pals have stayed true to him.

Every so often, Charlie loves going back to his home in Woodbridge to get away from the Busted mania. He sits by the river and watches the world go by while he catches up with his thoughts.

Matt is still really close to his Molesey mates and makes sure he goes back whenever he can to chill out with them.

He even gave them a credit in *A Present for Everyone.*

Matt: "It's been wicked since I've been in Busted, but I miss my friends and family. I get to see my mum now and then, but only for an hour before I have to shoot off again. I miss my mates, too. They were a big part of my life and now I hardly ever see them."

Charlie never forgets a birthday. He checks with his mum every so often to make sure he gets the dates of his brothers' birthdays right.

James loves going back to see his family. He reckons his little brother Chris changes every time he sees

him, because he's growing up so fast. Charlie says his friends have been cool about the superstar lifestyle he now has – "They're really happy for me, and I see them whenever I can."

Did you know?

• Matt has a friend called Shaggy who looks forward to having a poo! Matt reckons you could set your watch by his toilet habits.

• When James's mum moved his bed, she found about 1,000 bogeys stuck to the wall because he used to wipe them there. Gross!

WHO'S YOUR BEST MATE?

Is your ideal evening staying in with mates and a good movie?

Do you and your mates sport the skater look?

Would you describe yoursel as up-front and cheeky?

START

Is your best mate wild and mischievous?

Are you pretty good at being tidy around the house?

Is your best mate a bit of a brainbox on the quiet?

Are you thought of as the cute one in y our group of friends?

Are you always described as 'the loud one' by your mates?

Do you get told off for being cheeky at school?

Are you a bit of a practical joker when you're out with your mates?

Would you say you were a bit of a Britney fan?

Is your best mate a bit of a flirt?

YES / NO (path labels)

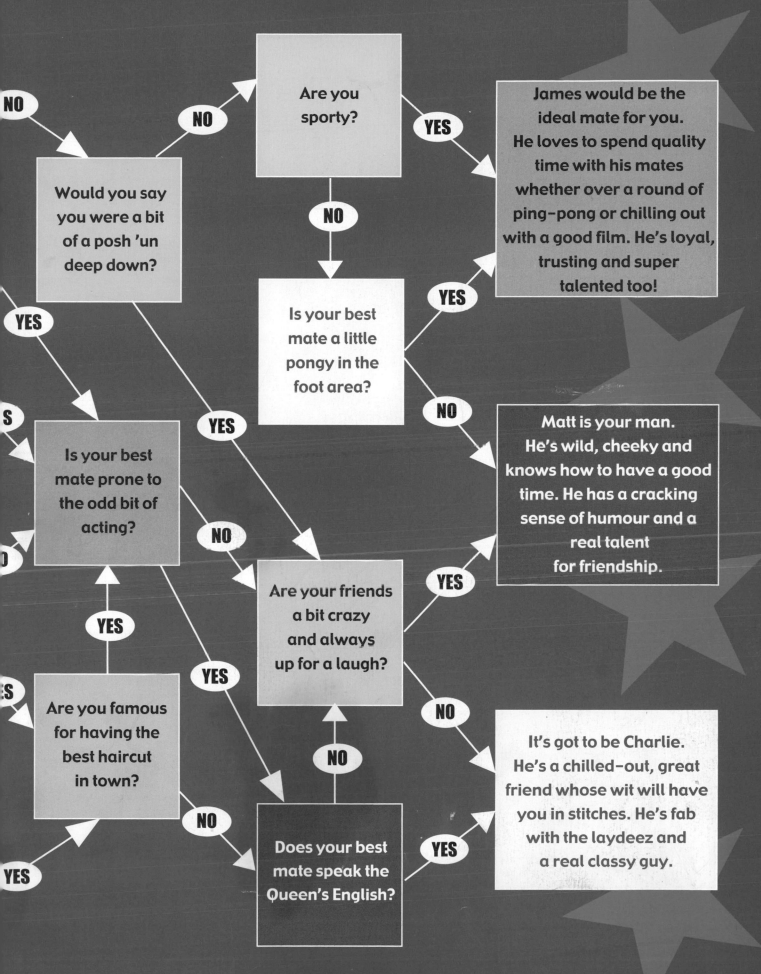

NO

NO

Are you sporty?

YES

James would be the ideal mate for you. He loves to spend quality time with his mates whether over a round of ping-pong or chilling out with a good film. He's loyal, trusting and super talented too!

Would you say you were a bit of a posh 'un deep down?

NO

YES

YES

Is your best mate a little pongy in the foot area?

YES

S

Is your best mate prone to the odd bit of acting?

YES

NO

NO

Matt is your man. He's wild, cheeky and knows how to have a good time. He has a cracking sense of humour and a real talent for friendship.

YES

ES

Are you famous for having the best haircut in town?

YES

Are your friends a bit crazy and always up for a laugh?

YES

NO

YES

NO

NO

It's got to be Charlie. He's a chilled-out, great friend whose wit will have you in stitches. He's fab with the laydeez and a real classy guy.

YES

Does your best mate speak the Queen's English?

YES

WHO'S YOUR TRUE LOVE?

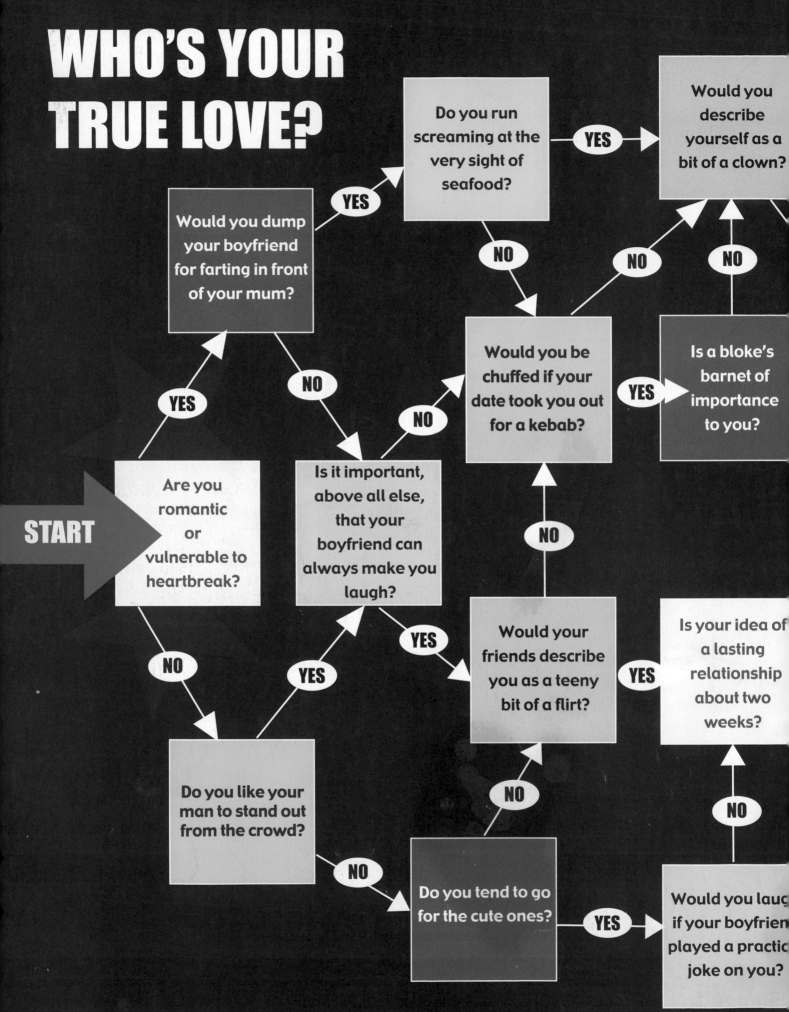

START

Are you romantic or vulnerable to heartbreak?

— YES → Would you dump your boyfriend for farting in front of your mum?

— NO → Do you like your man to stand out from the crowd?

Would you dump your boyfriend for farting in front of your mum?
— YES → Do you run screaming at the very sight of seafood?
— NO → Is it important, above all else, that your boyfriend can always make you laugh?

Do you run screaming at the very sight of seafood?
— YES → Would you describe yourself as a bit of a clown?
— NO → Would you be chuffed if your date took you out for a kebab?

Is it important, above all else, that your boyfriend can always make you laugh?
— YES →
— NO → Would you be chuffed if your date took you out for a kebab?

Would you be chuffed if your date took you out for a kebab?
— YES → Is a bloke's barnet of importance to you?
— NO → Would you describe yourself as a bit of a clown?

Is a bloke's barnet of importance to you?
— NO → Would you describe yourself as a bit of a clown?

Do you like your man to stand out from the crowd?
— YES →
— NO → Do you tend to go for the cute ones?

Do you tend to go for the cute ones?
— YES → Would you laugh if your boyfriend played a practical joke on you?
— NO → Would your friends describe you as a teeny bit of a flirt?

Would your friends describe you as a teeny bit of a flirt?
— YES → Is your idea of a lasting relationship about two weeks?
— NO →

Is your idea of a lasting relationship about two weeks?
— NO → Would you laugh if your boyfriend played a practical joke on you?

Would you laugh if your boyfriend played a practical joke on you?

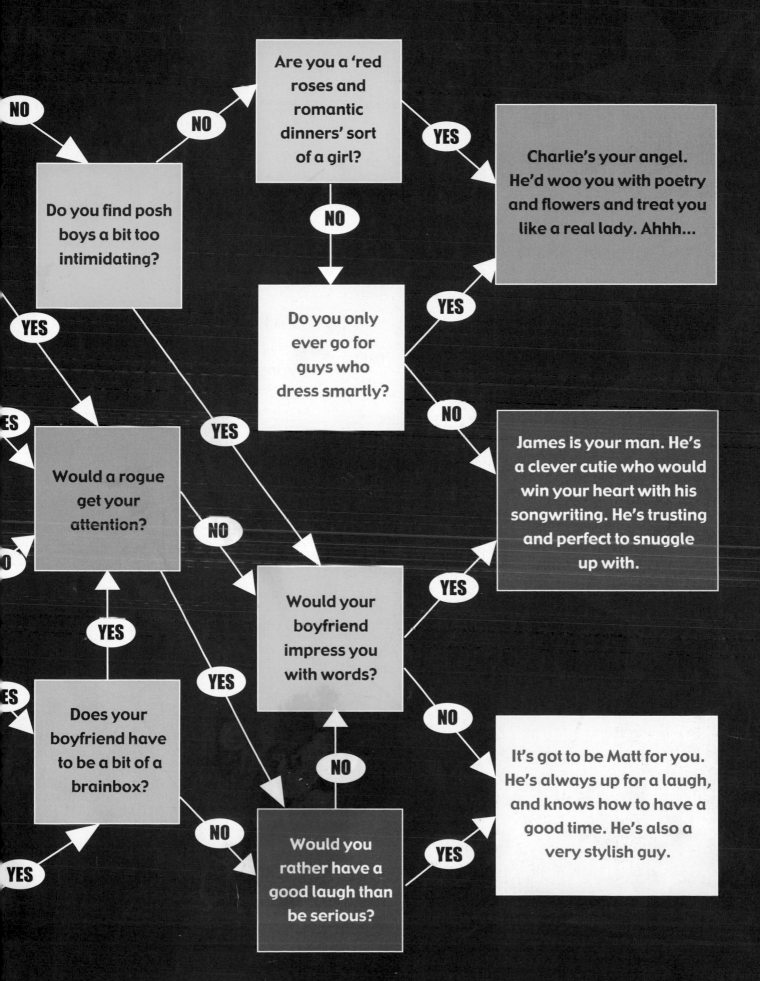

NO

NO

Are you a 'red roses and romantic dinners' sort of a girl?

YES

Charlie's your angel. He'd woo you with poetry and flowers and treat you like a real lady. Ahhh...

Do you find posh boys a bit too intimidating?

NO

YES

Do you only ever go for guys who dress smartly?

YES

YES

NO

ES

James is your man. He's a clever cutie who would win your heart with his songwriting. He's trusting and perfect to snuggle up with.

O

Would a rogue get your attention?

NO

YES

YES

Would your boyfriend impress you with words?

YES

ES

YES

Does your boyfriend have to be a bit of a brainbox?

NO

NO

It's got to be Matt for you. He's always up for a laugh, and knows how to have a good time. He's also a very stylish guy.

YES

NO

Would you rather have a good laugh than be serious?

YES

TV MOMENTS
BUSTED

In just one month, the Busted boys clocked up more TV performances than most bands get in a whole year, with performances and interviews all over the place.

One Saturday in April, the lads appeared on three TV shows in one day. It's a tiring schedule, but somebody's got to do it!

Top of the Pops, Top of the Pops Saturday, CD:UK, Diggin' It, Popworld and *T4* are just a few of the shows Busted have graced with their presence over the last twelve months. They have belted out 'Air Hostess', 'Who's David' and other smash hits to massive studio audiences.

Veteran celeb interviewer Jonathan Ross put the trio through their paces when they appeared on his Friday night show. He teased James for wearing shorts, Charlie for being so tall, and then got Matt to diss Simon Cowell in front of the nation.

Playing live on TV is not always possible, however much the boys might want to – "It means so much to us to play live, but it's sometimes literally impossible," says Charlie. "You can either be on the show and not play live, or not on the show, and it's stupid to turn down that big a TV show. So, when we can play live, we do."

Matt had a bizarre experience on Frank Skinner's show when Miss Mackenzie, the teacher who inspired the song 'What I Go To School For', made a surprise visit. Needless to say, Matt was just a little embarrassed. "She's so lovely," Matt says. "It must be so embarrassing for her. Even more embarrassing for me, though!"

Matt admits he's been hungover on just about every Saturday morning show he's ever done. And that's a lot of shows.

When the lads first started going on TV, they made a beeline for the babe-alicious presenters. "Whenever we'd see a fit presenter, we'd all play a game – who could be the most outrageously flirty person. You had to make sure you kept touching the presenter's knee or remark on how good-looking she was." Lucky ladies!

All three boys have sworn on television, much to the dismay of presenters.

The other game played by the Busted boys on TV is trying to slip the oddest words into interviews, words like Pikachu (Matt's phrase for a naughty person) or Stoopid (which actually means good in Matt-speak).

Matt: "Being on *Top Of The Pops* is a dream come true."

Charlie (on *Top Of The Pops*): "It's like a gig, because there's an audience. And we went on after David Bowie who was pre-recording a song. That was unreal."

James: "Performing live on TV or on tour is the best bit of being in Busted."

IMAGE CONSCIOUS
BUSTED

Nobody can touch the boys when it comes to style. They are trendsetters of the highest order. So what is their secret?

Charlie, the posh one

Charlie just gets smarter and smarter! His taste has definitely matured over the last year and his clothes say he's a cut above the rest. When he hits the town, he tends to wear quirky designer suits. His favourite accessories include a leather tie and white rockabilly shoes, which he teams with smart jackets to sharpen up the whole look.

Even when he's dressing down, Charlie stands out, with bright T-shirts, hooded sweaters, trendy jeans and khaki jackets.

Charlie's mop always looks well-kept. During one interview, it was revealed that he takes the longest to get ready out of the Busted lads. It takes time to get his hair looking that good, or so he says!

Charlie's eyebrows are so famous that he has to pull a hat over them if he doesn't want to get recognized when he's out and about.

Matt, the funky, punky one

Matt is one stylish guy and now that he has cash to spend, he's sharper than a knife.

The look for Matt is usually slightly punky and bad-boy. He's into slogan-heavy designer T-shirts and baggy trousers. His trademark this year was trucker caps, and he often wears leather jackets or scruffed up blazers to impress the babes. Even when he's lounging about, Matt looks cool in a pair of Pierre Cardin pyjama bottoms.

Our favourite practical joker certainly has a sense of humour about his appearance. Matt was not afraid of dressing like a bride in the 'Crashed the Wedding' video, and check out the faces he can pull!

Matt's not afraid to try new things. He wears eyeliner and hopes it will catch on for boys.

His hair is the most revered barnet in pop circles these days. He won the Top Pop Mop prize at the *Smash Hits* Awards, beating off competition from the rest of celebrityville with his luscious locks.

James, the skater boy

James is definitely into the casual, cool look. His trademark look is baggy, long shorts with trainers, and funky T-shirts.

Don't be fooled into thinking he doesn't make an effort with his appearance though. James's clothes are often customized by stylists because he likes them to look a little different. Go-faster stripes are added and his shorts are often cut-offs from long trousers.

James reckons his best features are his teeth, because they're nice and white, but fans would say it's his cheeky grin and those big blue eyes.

The Busted entourage

The Busted boys are natural pin-ups, but every celebrity needs a bit of help to get their looks spot on for TV cameras. For photoshoots, the lads get a stylist's help with their clothes, and a hair and make-up artist makes sure they're groomed and gorgeous.

It can take hours for the lads to get ready for a video shoot, but it's all worth it. When the single comes out, there they are, looking far too good to be true on your TV screen.

Did you know?

Charlie has a favourite pair of white shoes that he just loves because they make it easy for him to run around and jump about on stage. He had a bit of a panic during a show in Cardiff when he realized he'd left them in his hotel room. Luckily somebody ran back and managed to get them to him just three songs into the show. Phew, panic over!

James has a pair of lucky pants that he was wearing when Busted signed their first record deal. That's great, but he says he wears them all the time!

Matt (On his famous black-and-white mop): "No badgers inspired my hair. I nicked the style from a bass player in the Dum Dums (an old Indie rock band). Everybody says I've got the most original haircut they've ever seen. My mum hates it, though!"

James: "I have a habit of wearing the same socks for a long time. I need to buy some, but I haven't got the time to buy them." Make time, make time really soon!

Matt: "Before we were in Busted, James and I used to try getting into Chinawhite and Sugar Reef (London celeb nightclubs), and we were turned down every time. Now, we can stroll in with trainers and freaky hair."

SONGWRITING BUSTED

Okay, so everybody knows Busted rock. They are sexy, super-cool and their songs just keep getting better. However, the thing that really makes our trendy trio stand out from the crowd is the fact that they write their own material.

Their second album, *A Present for Everyone*, has been just that – a gift to all their fans. When you think they wrote it while they were on tour, you have to wonder, what's their secret?

James is best known for his songwriting skills, but it's a real team effort, and something the boys are really passionate about.

James: "Writing, for us, is a very important thing. We would like to work with different producers like N.E.R.D. and The Matrix, but we want to be the ones who write the songs."

Charlie says his main inspirations are still girls and movies. Good to see nothing's changed!

They might work together on their songs, but the lads admit they all have slightly different tastes themselves. Charlie was really into rock before he joined Busted, and he reckons that has been a good thing for the band. He and his brother Will wrote the ballad *Why* together, and Matt and James loved it so much they put it on *A Present for Everyone*. Matt loves writing and hearing fun songs, but what he really wants to write about is falling in love.

Despite all this, the band remain modest about their music.
James: "We don't claim to write music that changes people's lives." Many of their fans would disagree with that!

Here are a few fascinating snippets of info about some of the tracks on *A Present for Everyone:*

• 'Air Hostess': The lads love them. James was recently told off by an air hostess for mimicking her safety procedure hand movements, and Charlie reckons air hostesses on Virgin Airlines are the fittest.

• 'Crashed the Wedding': Matt's favourite bit in the song is the line, 'I stole my girl away from everybody gathered there that day'. "It's genius," he says. " 'Gathered there that day', it's what the vicar says!"

• 'Who's David': Described as a ready-made pop/rock classic, it was written while the band was on tour, and jumped to number one like a shot. The name David is nothing personal, though. James only chose it because it rhymed with 'invaded'.

• '3AM': Along with 'Air Hostess', this is one of Charlie's favourite tracks on *A Present for Everyone*.

• 'Fallin 4 You': Matt reckons it contains some very interesting Na-na-na's. So now you know!

• For 'Over Now', 'Nerdy' and 'Who's David', the boys commissioned a 24-piece string section, to add some magnificent orchestral flourishes.

SUCCESSOMETER

Track the real story of Busted's breakthrough on the meter of magic.

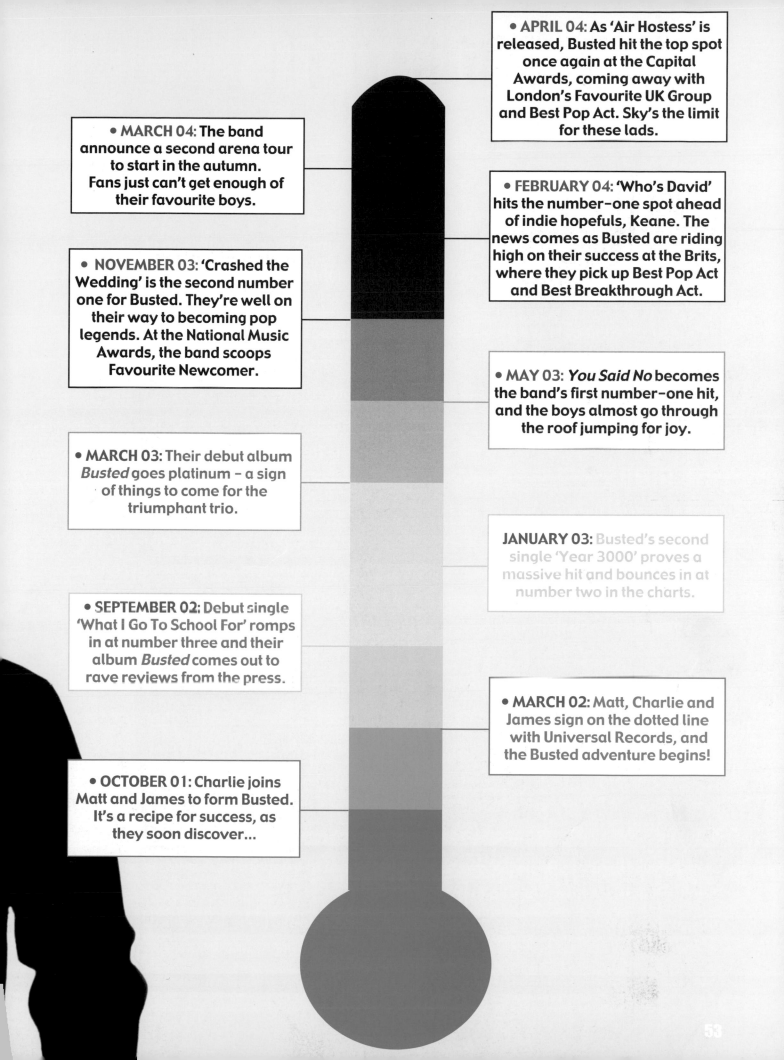

• **APRIL 04:** As 'Air Hostess' is released, Busted hit the top spot once again at the Capital Awards, coming away with London's Favourite UK Group and Best Pop Act. Sky's the limit for these lads.

• **MARCH 04:** The band announce a second arena tour to start in the autumn. Fans just can't get enough of their favourite boys.

• **FEBRUARY 04:** 'Who's David' hits the number-one spot ahead of indie hopefuls, Keane. The news comes as Busted are riding high on their success at the Brits, where they pick up Best Pop Act and Best Breakthrough Act.

• **NOVEMBER 03:** 'Crashed the Wedding' is the second number one for Busted. They're well on their way to becoming pop legends. At the National Music Awards, the band scoops Favourite Newcomer.

• **MAY 03:** *You Said No* becomes the band's first number-one hit, and the boys almost go through the roof jumping for joy.

• **MARCH 03:** Their debut album *Busted* goes platinum – a sign of things to come for the triumphant trio.

JANUARY 03: Busted's second single 'Year 3000' proves a massive hit and bounces in at number two in the charts.

• **SEPTEMBER 02:** Debut single 'What I Go To School For' romps in at number three and their album *Busted* comes out to rave reviews from the press.

• **MARCH 02:** Matt, Charlie and James sign on the dotted line with Universal Records, and the Busted adventure begins!

• **OCTOBER 01:** Charlie joins Matt and James to form Busted. It's a recipe for success, as they soon discover...

CELEBRITY STATUS
BUSTED

Being a sizzling hot property has some serious perks. The Busted boys are in demand with babes everywhere, and are regulars on the celebrity circuit. In this section, you'll find out how they really feel about fame and discover what they think are the best and worst bits of being the biggest new pop sensation on the planet.

The highs

James loves all the attention he gets from blushing babes. They're always giving him their phone numbers in the hope that he'll call. He has given millions of autographs and has even been known to sign bras!

Charlie's fab looks have earned him some top attention from girls. He literally gets jumped on by some of his fans. It's crazy!

James reckons the experience hasn't changed him, but it has changed his life – "If you look at all our lives before Busted and then look at them now, they're completely different," he says.

Matt is pleased with all the freebies – "We get all sorts of stuff sent to us," he says. "I must have a collection of about fifty-eight ties at home."

James is also getting mega amounts of cool post from fans. In one interview he said he liked Jaffa Cakes and now he gets them wherever he goes. But he reckons the best bit about being in Busted is all the opportunities it's given him – "We have access to so many great things and top people. Anything we want to do in the entertainment world, we now have a headstart," he says.

The boys are buzzing on their fame. They have got fans everywhere they go and they're loved by celebrities too! Everton striker Wayne Rooney came to their Manchester show and hung out with the lads afterwards. Together they took in a spot of the local nightlife. Wayne's a big fan of Busted and friends with all the boys.

Hollyoaks babe Jodie Albert, who plays the gorgeous Debbie Dean, was spotted out on the town with the threesome. Lucky girl!

Charlie got to go to the biggest event of the year – the rugby World Cup winners' homecoming dinner!

The lows

On the other hand, it's a tiring business being on the road so much. The boys hardly have a moment to themselves, what with songwriting, performing and travelling.

"Sometimes it's easy to forget you have a life outside the band," says James.

The trio all miss their families and their friends while they're away.

There's always masses going on around them – so much so that it gets a bit crazy.

Charlie lists the downsides as no time, no sleep, and getting the odd bit of stick from people who are jealous of his fabulous good looks and celebrity lifestyle.

But the Busted boys don't let this sort of thing get them down. They say they're proud to be a pop band and they love their loyal fans.

So, it's not bad being a Busted lad, after all!

BUSTED

Busted really are on top of the game when it comes to making videos. What with the use of cutting-edge technology, ultra-hip locations and awesome costumes, they deserve an Oscar! And it seems that Oscars are not too far from their minds...

Busted, the movie

The lads are already in talks about a movie, and they've got some very firm ideas about what they want, and what they don't want.

However, they are determined to ensure that they're part of the whole film production process – "We don't just want somebody to give us a script. We want to be involved with writing it too," Charlie explains.

And fans who are hoping to see the boys play themselves, a bit like in the S Club movie, could be disappointed – "It's not going to be in 'Busted World'," says James. Matt adds, "It's going to be like an English *American Pie* with us in it."

The boys have chosen some top Hollywood stars whom they'd like to work with – Edward Norton and Macaulay Culkin are favourites for the film.

There's no firm date for the film's release yet, but the boys are already writing, and it could be out as early as 2006. So there's plenty of time for you to choose your outfit for the premiere...

Busted, the videos

Meanwhile, the trio are having second thoughts about dressing as women for their future videos. Matt wore a fetching bride's outfit for the chart-topping single 'Crashed the Wedding', but he admits he's not in any hurry to repeat the stunt. After speaking to a friend about it, he found out that his mate didn't realize it was Matt, and said the band should have found a fitter-looking bride – "He seriously thought it was just some ugly extra that we'd stuck in there. I was like, 'How bad is that?'!"

James, however, was chuffed with the video for 'Crashed the Wedding' – "The idea for the song came from the movie *Wayne's World 2*, which was out ages ago, and there's a scene in it which inspired us to write this track," he says. "Making the video for it was crazy. We went totally over the top with the costume changes and scenes. It took twenty-four hours solid to shoot, and I ended up with latex stuck to my face from when I was dressed up as an old man."

Shooting secrets

What I Go To School For:
• Charlie had to sit under a blanket for three hours waiting for the rain to stop before he could shoot his fantasy scene – running through a field after Miss Mackenzie in his underwear!
• The production team had to buy 200 school ties for the extras in the video.
• James had to become an overnight expert in moonwalking.
• Matt had to fall out of the tree fifteen times.

Year 3000:
• The guy who plays Matt's older double in the video has also appeared as a wizard in a *Harry Potter* movie.
• The video cost £130,000 to make.

Sleeping With The Light On:
• The shoot took two days and was filmed in London. It took place near to an all girls' school, so there were just a few fans there!

ON TOUR BUSTED

Touring has been the name of the game for Busted this year. Their first arena tour was so spectacularly successful that they immediately announced another one in autumn 2004. Tickets sold out faster than you can say "We love Busted". It's hard work for Matt, James and Charlie, being on the road all year, but they're not complaining. Here are some of the perks which come with their touring lifestyle:

Bus stop

The Busted tour bus sleeps thirty-nine people. It's even got a luxury lounge and a jacuzzi in the back, so the boys can chill out in style even while they are on the move.

The trio have become good at entertaining themselves between shows. The top game on the Busted bus in 2004 was Connect 4. The lads all got totally addicted to it. And when they weren't beating each other at Connect 4, they were making the most of the Chopper bikes they were given to take on tour.

Of course, there's fun to be had on the tour bus, but according to Matt he tries to keep his practical joking to a minimum – "I used to [play jokes all the time], but Charlie and James really don't appreciate them," he says. "There's only so many times you can chuck water at each other!"

James admits he can't get enough of the tour bus. He says he loves being on it. He even chose to get the ferry to Dublin rather than the plane, so he could stay on it. "It's a complete chill-out zone," he says. "You get to watch DVDs and sleep – two of my favourite pastimes." He even reckons it helps to get the creative juices flowing – "We'll party after each gig but it's always good to write on tour. You find you write a couple of songs in the evening."

Each venue they go to is different, but the boys always have everything they need laid on for them. However, a word of advice, the dressing room is not the best place to meet the boys. "We don't get a chance to chill out there. You come off stage, put a towel around your neck and shoot off to meet the tour bus," says Matt.

Tour titbits

The tour set had about sixteen songs in it, so the boys were playing for around an hour and twenty minutes.

The stage sets for the gigs were specially designed for the boys, with loads of cool moving screens and plenty of room for them to run and jump around in true Busted style.

There was a drum duo each night – a play off with two sets of drums.

Matt: "It's been completely mad, we've been all around the world. I don't think I've ever looked forward to anything more than going on tour. Playing live is the best thing about being in a band."

Charlie also lists being on tour as one of his favourite things. He hasn't even been put off by an onstage accident, when he jumped off the stage at the end of one show and ended up going headfirst into a metal barrier. Fortunately he wasn't hurt.

Charlie's fall wasn't the only hitch on the tour. In Belfast during a performance of 'You Said No', one of the pyrotechnics unexpectedly exploded, giving everyone on stage the fright of their lives!
Nobody said it was easy being a pop star...

QUICK QUIZ

If you've read this book from cover to cover, you should know everything there is to know about Busted. Test yourself with this quick quiz, and then check your answers on page 61.

1. Which of the Busted boys was told off for throwing a toaster out of a window?

2. Who is a sucker for onion gravy?

3. Who and what was Hump–Three?

4. What was the favourite game aboard the Busted tour bus?

5. When they first met Charlie, what nationality did James and Matt think he was?

6. What did James's mum find stuck on his bedroom wall?

7. How many girls does Charlie say he's kissed?

8. How many people can the Busted tour bus sleep?

9. Which Busted boy hates fish?

10. What happened to James when he accidentally spat into his microphone?

11. Which bird would Matt like to be?

12. Why was the name David chosen for the song 'Who's David'?

13. What did Matt buy for his mum?

14. Where did Charlie go to school?

15. Who is the messiest man in Busted?

16. Who dressed up as a bride in the 'Crashed the Wedding' video?

17. How old was Charlie when he got his first electric guitar?

18. What did Matt do to earn sweets from his nan?

19. How much would you have to pay James to drink his own wee?

20. Who wrote the song 'Why'?

TOMORROW BUSTED

It's been a scorching twelve months for Busted. They've broken just about every rule, record and damsel's heart. And there's so much more to come...

• A Busted film is definitely on the cards. The boys have started working on material for the venture.

• Justin Timberlake is going to be getting very pally with Busted – if the lads have their way. They want to do a duet with him.

• James reckons Busted are going to be around for a long time to come, so there's no need for the hankies just yet – "I think we've got a bit more longevity!" he says.

• Matt can't imagine life without the band any more – "At the moment people out there are loving it. I don't want to think of the time when they don't any more," he says.

• Charlie has fallen in love with California. He wants to get a house in the hills and spend six months of the year there (sob!).

• Matt is determined to keep the fun coming – "I love writing fun songs," he says. Though he also wants to write about falling in love. Awww!

• Charlie reckons that in the future it is essential for Busted to stay true to the high standards they've set in *A Present for Everyone* – "That's the sound that I think is best for Busted," he says.

• James says he's still on a learning curve, and he's keen to start writing for film soundtracks, being a bit of a movie lover.

• Charlie would love to get into films and boy, is he going the right way about it. Who wouldn't want to see those chiselled features on the big screen?

Answers to the quiz on page 60

1. Matt
2. Matt
3. James's pet hamster
4. Connect 4
5. Dutch
6. Bogeys
7. One hundred
8. Thirty-nine
9. Charlie
10. He got electrocuted
11. A peregrine falcon
12. Because it rhymed with 'invaded'
13. A Ford Mondeo
14. Uppingham Public School
15. Charlie
16. Matt
17. Ten years old
18. He picked up dog poo
19. £30,000
20. Charlie and his brother Will